FLIGHT

T0345806

SUNKEN GARDEN POETRY AT HILL-STEAD MUSEUM

Hill-Stead Museum's renowned Sunken Garden Poetry Festival is a unique outdoor arts event located on the grounds of the Hill-Stead estate, a National Historic Landmark in the heart of Farmington, Connecticut. The community cherishes this annual series of readings and concerts in the informal outdoor setting. Visitors can come early to tour the museum's world-class Impressionist art collection, walk the trails, or attend the prelude conversations with headlining poets. Picnics are welcome, and guests bring their own chairs and blankets to relax among the flowerbeds in the historic Sunken Garden, surrounded by eight-foot stone walls and the sounds of nature.

Out of the festival have grown competitions, year-round workshops and events, and educational outreach to area high schools. And while centered at Hill-Stead—with its beautiful views, Colonial Revival house, and superb art collection—Sunken Garden Poetry now engages an ever-wider audience through a growing online presence, a video library of past readings, the online journal *Theodate*, and an annual chapbook prize, with the winning group of poems co-published by Tupelo Press.

For a calendar of readings and other events, see: www.hillstead.org/sunken-garden-poetry-festival/.

SUNKEN GARDEN POETRY PRIZE

2014
We Practice for It by Ted Lardner
Selected by Mark Doty

2015
Fountain and Furnace by Hadara Bar-Nadav
Selected by Peter Stitt

2016
Feed by Suzanne Parker
Selected by Jeffrey Levine and Cassandra Cleghorn

2017
Ordinary Misfortunes by Emily Jungmin Yoon
Selected by Maggie Smith

2018
Flight by Chaun Ballard
Selected by Major Jackson

FLIGHT

CHAUN BALLARD

T|P TUPELO PRESS   North Adams, Massachusetts

Library of Congress Cataloging-in-Publication Data
Names: Ballard, Chaun, 1980– author.
Title: Flight / Chaun Ballard.
Other titles: Sunken Garden Poetry Prize ; 2018.
Description: North Adams, Massachusetts : Tupelo Press, [2018] | Series:
  Sunken Garden Poetry Prize ; 2018
Identifiers: LCCN 2018025836 | ISBN 9781946482136 (pbk. original : alk. paper)
Subjects: LCSH: Families–Poetry. | Race–Poetry.
Classification: LCC PS3602.A621124 A6 2018 | DDC 811/.6–dc23

Cover and text designed by Ann Aspell.
Cover art: *Come Fly With Me* by Karen Powell. Acrylics on canvas, 24 x 24 inches. Copyright © 2018.
Used with permission of the artist (http://www.powelldesign.com/).

First paperback edition: July 2018.

Tupelo Press
P.O. Box 1767, 243 Union Street, Eclipse Mill, Loft 305
North Adams, Massachusetts 01247
(413) 664–9611 / editor@tupelopress.org
www.tupelopress.org

Tupelo Press is an award-winning independent literary press that publishes fine fiction, nonfiction, and poetry in
books that are a joy to hold as well as read. Tupelo Press is a registered 501(c)(3) nonprofit organization, and we rely
on public support to carry out our mission of publishing extraordinary work that may be outside the realm of large
commercial publishers. Financial donations are welcome and are tax deductible.

To those we have loved.

CONTENTS

FLIGHT

Midway

So now when the ghost asks me
my age, I say, *I'm stomach over*
the waistband; I'm button up
and neck-tied; I'm shoes no longer
the last squawking on hard wooden
floors; I'm totem pole carved with faces
of the past; I'm apple for lunch, walnuts,
and pleasant dinners; I'm red cross
bloodletting and good credit; I'm
my father in that faded polaroid
taken somewhere in California;
I'm high school reunion almost
checked the box: maybe; I'm electric
slide and Jesus music, hallelujahs
and morning glory; I'm open
book and lamp light; I'm Achilles
if he lived during the Renaissance;
I'm nearly in danger of not being
a danger; old enough to say,
you were good and died young.

GAZELLES

We often travel in clusters. In flight like wild birds.
We often rest where we find rest, sleep where we find
sleep, and, yes, the two are different. We often drink
when we should drink. We often drink when we shouldn't.

And our young (too young) are too young to understand
thirst as a verb, thirst as a movement, so they make a fuss
of the rain. And the rain falls seldom. And the rain falls
heavy. And the rain falls and falls until it is more than just

rain. And the rain is a paradox. And the rain
is a riddle. And the rain is a metaphor. And the rain is
a shelter. And the rain is just rain. And the rains,
to a practiced gazelle, are lamentations when absent.

And our young are too young. And our young
are young runners. And our young are multitudes:
a watering hole's convenience. They walk where we walk.
They drink where we drink. They rest where we rest.

They run when we run.

GOLDEN SHOVEL

after William Carlos Williams

Our neighborhood of stolen bikes, backyards, and so-
called conditions of standard living (where nothing was much),
Papa would drive up, reverse, and parallel into his spot like the spot depends
on the smoothness of his return. Wednesdays upon
the red brick column we leaned, porch heavy and lethargic like a
scene to be duplicated the next week. I would eyeball the red
brick weighed between brothers, brushstroke my hands over the worn flaws. And a wheel,
accompanied by other wheels, would always come to a halt whenever a child would barrow
across the one-way like he was tethered to a friend or a loose ball glazed
in bacon grease and popcorn oil. Sometimes those headlights froze on a naked dime with-
out renaming a street, avenue, or lane, but too often they did not. Rain
was the usual culprit fingered in a series of lineups. Ice water,
the other that shot mothers out of starting blocks, Jackie-Joyner-Kersee beside
their child lying broken in the
road. From our red brick America, this was our rerun, our white
picket fence, our Wednesday evenings Papa made it home, jivin' he saw a man about a duck.

Twelve Ways of Looking at Darkness

after Wallace Stevens

1.

I was bred in the darkness
out of pant stank & memory

Papa held the keys to the x-y
while Momma flowered
like a child under the moon

2.

I slid out of her darkness
head first with bloodshot eyes
& skin that wouldn't take in the light

3.

like candlelight
we learned to count our days
in darkness

4.

the blacker the berry — Momma would say
is the dark-darker-darkness
the kind whose outer flesh does not respond
to anything less than magenta

5.

I've known the whites of too many
eyes in passion & flame

those whose souls eternalize everything
even the darkness

6.

when Papa was away
Momma's roost wasn't the wiser
so (of course) the two could not be reconciled
& neither could our dark nest

7.

we admire everything brilliant
star & moon
flame & angel

never once have I heard one say
how lovely the dark is

8.

I adorn the head of Cushitic
thick-napped necks Afros
du-rags & wave caps

even Alexander turned his face
toward Egypt when he saw our multitudes
layered in the darkness

9.

God said *Let there be light* & there was light
& God saw that the light was good

& they would have believed us—
if only I hadn't coveted your light & you
my darkness

10.

even if I left this section blank
(which I am considering)
the em dash would still spill dark
onto the page

11.

eleven ways to say darkness:

aphotic / obscure / ill-intended / inhumane / indistinguishable /
somber / murky / nothingness / Cimmerian / after the earth has been cast out
or swallowed / nebulous—if anyone or anything else remains

12.

my shadow is a child

How We Are Made to Feel Small

I remember the feeling I had after September 11th, after seeing
a photo of Michael Jordan watching the footage of two buildings,
two planes, two worlds colliding into a mess of ash and rebar.
I remember it like the first time I relearned I was black:
It was summer of '91; I was ten. I was running through the apartment
complex looking for bad guys to fake shoot with my plastic gun.
I was Bruce Willis. The apartment complex was a scene
from *Die Hard*. I remember the feel of wind as it caught my shirt:
how safe it must have felt there, how my lungs trusted it, filled themselves
with it. My legs, cutting through it like propellers on a plane,
like spokes on the bike I did not need to apprehend my suspects.
I had a plastic gun, a fake badge. Together they were truth. Truth
was what they taught in primary school. Truth was when they asked us
what we wanted to be, and some answered president, fireman, police
officer. I never wanted to be president or a fireman, that's the truth.
I wanted to be John McClane. I wanted to be Bruce Willis in a scene
from *Die Hard*. I wanted to save the city and sum up the day
in a catchphrase: *Yippee-ki-yay, motha*—before my mother called me
home. Outside LeBron James's LA home, someone spray-painted
the n-word on his gate. LeBron's response was, *No matter how
much money you have, no matter how famous you are, no matter how
many people admire you, being black in America is tough*. It was summer
of '91 when I learned this truth. Some truths are hard. Some truths are not
whole truths. Like the day my teacher invited the officer into our class-
room and told us his job was to protect and serve us. We believed her
because she was our teacher. We believed her because he stood there,

ten feet tall. I was ten when the officer stopped me, ten
when they stopped Rodney King. Wind was still filling my shirt,
my legs: propellers on a plane before he brought me to a full stop—
before he examined my plastic gun, before *You better spray-paint an orange*
tip on that, before *I almost shot you*. My junior year in university,
a far cry from California, my Texas teammates banged on my door,
yelling, *Turn on your TV, turn on your TV*. What I saw was like the rebirth
of a phoenix un-ashing—afterwards, Michael Jordan (some basketball player's
LeBron James today) staring into a TV screen, small, like the rest of us.
The summer of '91 was the summer I stopped carrying a fake badge
and plastic gun. It was the summer I stopped believing I was Bruce Willis.
It was the summer we turned on our TV screens to find Rodney King
clubbed into asphalt. It was a hard truth to come by, a hard truth to be woken to,
like the scene of a black child staring into the business end
of what I want to believe is a cruel joke—

Running in My Sleep

When I wake, she describes
       everything but the dream. She describes

my breathing:
       the double-double-one,

the husband seated on the floor
       behind his wife at Lamaze class.

She describes the moment
       after the bride removes the pomp and circumstance and

the groom enters the peak of himself
       with each creak into climax.

She describes *la petite mort*, the little death:
       the laborious hours of lung work

the body must do for a child
       entering this world.

She describes the sand
       of man's first breath.

She describes the purse-lipped daredevil:
       the hype of superstardom

doubling inside himself the way fallen angels exit heaven.
        She describes

the hunters arrayed in flak jackets,
        knowing

they don't have to but must kill.
        She describes the thunderbird overcome by

his shadowy absence over
        Thunderbird Falls.

She describes the hurricaned waters,
        the paleotempestologist recording its fury,

the earth's plea to no contest.
        She describes the pattering of feet just before

the dead leap into heaven.
        She describes the ataxia,

the asphyxia,
        the apotheosis of man.

Dear Basketball: A Posthumous Letter from St. Louis

with lines from Kobe Bryant's retirement poem

I can't quite remember who made the first move
or who fantasized about who. I knew nothing
of garbage cans, game-winning threes— unless
you count the fish sticks I tossed to the dogs
with an overwhelming chance it
might be swallowed by one of the two— &
who was I fooling? I was a terrible shot
(plus the dogs ignored
the fish-like substance, deemed it
inedible before seeking out Papa's thick black
socks to chew, after his nine
to five, after his
holiday pay, after over- time times time-&-a-half multiplied
by two). I'd be lying if I said I
loved you or even knew
you during those days when I was
chasing down the legend of Oz, the
gold-glove wizard himself—
I practically bled Red Bird National
League. Never once did I search for you,
nor sought you through a bucket pulled next to
the bedroom door for an easy bank-shot
of two—not a love deep for you. At eight-
years-old, I was burning down garbage bins,

a neighbor's garage, stripping emblems off
cars, a breaking & entering
or two — never for you.   I ran because
I could, because   I had to,
because the hustle & the police
stayed up late.   You know the routine:
If someone takes off running,
you take off, too — &   after
a mile or so or   two, two, two-o-o-o:
Why the hell we runnin'?
Somebody finally speaks up for you.   I prayed
hurt, sweat down to the kneecaps like   *Someone, please!*
I did everything but follow you —
I'd give anything to bring you back.   *My heart can't take*
the pounding, my mind can't take
the grind, my body knows it's time to say   *goodbye:*
hallowed be thy name is true.
I know,   I can't savor
the past in the moment. We will always be
one shot shy of each other — Papa's rolled-up
sock for me won't do. The garbage can near
the door I will leave for   another —
                                                     it doesn't matter

who.

Using the Laws of Motion to Explain Ferguson

from the Columbia Electronic Encyclopedia

1. First Law

a body at rest tends to remain
      at rest
a body in motion tends to remain
      in motion
at a constant speed in a straight line

unless acted on
by an outside force

2. Second Law

the acceleration a of a mass m
      by an unbalanced force F

is directly proportional
      to the force

and inversely proportional to the mass
or a [knee-jerk reaction] = F [ired shots] / m [ichael brown]

3. Third Law

for every action there is an equal
      and opposite reaction

the total momentum of a system
of bodies
not acted on by an external force
remains constant
(see conservation laws in physics)

4. [Limitations]

~~newton's laws of motion~~
~~together~~

~~with his laws of gravitation~~
~~provide a satisfactory basis~~

~~for the explanation~~
~~of motion~~

~~of everyday macroscopic objects~~
~~under everyday conditions~~
however

when applied to extremely high speeds
or extremely small objects

~~newton's~~
laws break down

ANTHEM

So it's off to the devil
        you know. The devil
you believe in. The one
        you run to like a believer. Him,
you believe will save you like
        the Pitbull,
the Rottweiler you keep
        chained in your backyard
at a safe distance.
        The one you approach with calm in your voice.
The one you make visible your empty hands.
        The one you hope will receive you in faith,
in good conscience.
        The one you hope good still serves his memory.
As you pray you will not fall into song.
        As you say, *I have only run out of gas.*

•

As they wash your back
        clean of fresh wounds,
let no one say,
        Only the guilty run.
The innocent don't run.
        Only the guilty, they run away.

•

And who are we to make your song meaningless?

•

So to the devil we know, we go,
          locked-arm. We kiss
knees to the ground
          to honor the departed.
And someone will make this about flags,
          and someone will make this about football,
while we, the living, are still dying,
          while another June-skinned body scores a goal.

WE SING

and no one dies.
Here we say:

he put up quite a song—
lovely how he sang it:

live:
on screen:

on radio—
the event was celebrated in song:

in the beat of a wing.
Smooth as a flight of evening sparrows.

Here, when a shot fires
and whistles,

we say:
he burst into song

we say:
in the act of singing

we say:
that one there

can be bought
for a hymn —

for the rhythm
you hear

and keep in
your head.

Like that
of blown leaves —

the nearness
of the nameless

buzz
or hum

made by a pair
of hives.

Ghazal

I envisioned myself one day becoming a black hole—
if ever a man aimed his side-arm at me to cut me off from being black: whole.

I'd probably ask God: *What will it take for me to breathe the same air?*
He'd probably say: *Now that, my dear child, will take a whole lot of black holes.*

I've watched mothers reach through time continuums, lineated voids, to find their young
dearly departing into sky, pulling what's left of light nail-deep into black holes.

Do I need to know much about astronomy to understand the gravity
of this situation: whole communities shovel & night-veil, gazing into black holes?

When newspapers called him stellar, I didn't fault them. How were they to know his teammates were
scientists & mathematicians who believed every ball passed was a ball lost to a black hole?

To every soul there is a given number of championships we must call *celebration*
or *survival* before we top-end malt liquor bottles heavy into black. Holes

(by definition) are hollow; therefore, we are sought to fill them
with consciousness, with earth, with shadow, with ourselves—with anything black. Whole-

sale is how we live our lives, & you ask why do I speak in metaphors. *Because we are metaphors*, I say.
Matter & mass, superstars fleeing light, always dying, always black: holes.

(More) Alternate Names for Black Boys

after Danez Smith

18. werewolves in daylight
19. embers without wings
20. orwellian sonnets
21. bones of obsidian & flint
22. aim & fire's love child
23. rorschach ink blot
24. bulletproof—
25. no proof—
26. poof!—he gone
27. ashes to dust
28. white sheets & closed curtains
29. abracadaver
30. abrakaboom!
31. —
32. forgotten

How to Make the World Beautiful

Take the scent
of a chalk-lined morning.

Sift it into grains.
Grind them into people:

bring them back.
Stuff them in your pocket

when no one is looking.
Keep them on your person

(at all times).
Dig a hole in the dirt

when it is known
a village resides

at your hip.
Unname them

forgotten —
call them

gardens,
watch them grow.

PANTOUM ON THE PRESIDENTIAL ELECTION

in Saudi Arabia

Fall is tolerable here in Jeddah.
Still, I keep the AC on. My middle-high
students are keeping me up-to-date
on the presidential election.

Still, I keep the AC on. The middle-high
faithfully follow the news, I mean down
to the minute. *What do you think about the presidential
election?* they ask. *Who do you want to win?*

Faithfully following the news, my students
believe Hillary can't be trusted. *Trump
is crazy,* they say. *Who do you want to win?*
Abdulrahman retells a joke,

believes Hillary can't be trusted, and Trump
hates Muslims and Mexicans.
Abdulrahman retells a joke,
If Hillary and Trump are in a boat—

Hates Muslims and Mexicans, I think to myself.
The teacher in me wants to respond: *Hate is such a strong word.*
But I allow him to continue. *If Hillary and Trump are in a boat
and it capsizes, who survives?*

The teacher in me wants to respond: *Hate is such a strong word.*
My wife sends me a message, says colleagues are offering condolences.
Abdulrahman presses, *If it capsizes, Mr. Chaun, who survives?*
I want to say I don't understand the question.

Why are people offering condolences?
My colleague interrupts, asks to use the AC remote.
I want to say I don't understand the question.
Admin has emailed a request for early contract renewal.

My colleague takes the AC remote, heads for the door.
My school director leans against the doorway.
Admin has emailed a request for early contract renewal,
but that's not why he's here. He says Trump is in the lead.

My school director is Canadian.
We could shoot the breeze about anything on any day,
but that's not why he's here. *Trump is in the lead,* he says.
My colleague who has taken the AC remote is Jordanian.

We could shoot the breeze about anything, on any day.
Trust me, we can go on like this forever.
My colleague who has taken the AC remote, the Jordanian,
turns around, says, *What do you think about this man?*

Trust me, I say, *We can go on about him forever.*
But the school has a shortage of AC remotes.
What I think about this man
is the last thing on my mind,

especially when I know AC remotes are in high demand.
Abdulrahman lingers. His retelling still an open end,
and patience is the last thing on his mind.
My wife tells me everyone is offering condolences.

I want to say I don't get the joke.
I want to ask, *Who died?*

My Being-Black Dilemma

My students are learning how to make America. *Great…Again?*
one says to me (his literature teacher). *Yes*, I reply, *make America great.* Again

and again, he complains, recreates cities, states, river systems, borders on the map.
This isn't social studies. No, I say, *this is context. Now continue making America great.* Again

the Civil War is fought, the bloody lesson of a nation burned into youth. I teach them
North vs. South, industry vs. agriculture, but all they hear is "make America great." Again,

as if somewhere in the South, engaged in battle, a stone-like pupil will emerge, horseless,
to say he's not seeing the connection. *Make America great*, again

I say to him. *This is context. The story is difficult. The views, however visible, complex.*
If we are to engage in meaningful dialogue, understand: making America great again

adds substance to the story. We are reading "An Occurrence at Owl Creek Bridge,"
and again Peyton Farquhar is to be hanged for the cause: to make America great. Again,

I must take my students through the grueling process of strangulation, how a man's mind travels
even until death, even until America is made great. Again,

I must teach them to pity the plantation owner: "a civilian and student of hanging." I must teach
them to look at the man as a man (not his cause or ideals) to make America great.

Rendition

You've heard the story
of the boy with waxed wings

who flew too close to the sun
who was himself a son

to a father a mother
whom he blanketed with light

You probably read the story
or at least heard it as I did

a son of the sun
his permanent silhouette

his glowing aftermath
the sorrow of his knowing

blood of waxed wings
his plunge into a gray earth—

Well I'm not here to tell you that story
I'm not here to tell you a tale

of a labyrinth's secret
I'm not here to sell you the hell

of a concrete prison
or its conditions

I wish only to describe
his flight

how beautiful
his wings

how in the heart of a blood-orange sun
Icarus   lives

A Love Poem

Michael Brown as an old man

He entered the park's archway / hands withered like the leaves of November / shuffling beneath his feet / finding and losing them- / selves like the memory / of one / who pauses every few steps to admire the buildings / that had once been trees / and searches the sun / until he finds himself lost and lingering / like a stray to the public bench / where he removes his cap / balances his cane on his leg / and examines the faces of strangers / as one would / a map

When I found him there / he had already begun speaking of rivers / going on about the weather / seasons / and the earth's axial tilt / how it was perfect like the curve of his Cardinal's cap / or the hem of his wife's ballroom dress / He complimented the sun / and spoke highly of the moon's obsession with shooting stars / how he whispered dark matter / into the celestial ear of open space / how the shadow of the earth passes over a smile as a light wind / lifting silver leaves

like embers from their place / and he spoke of how / the same happiness can remind / a man of sorrow / and how both reminded him of his bride / in the garden / and the first dance they had ever danced

UNFINISHED SONNET

for Donnell "Don-Don" Romaine Jury

You strolled through the club that night, not mob deep, just a few
boys who wanted to fine-tune rhythm's beat beneath pleat
& skirt until your pelvis caked sore. You had a few drinks,
you & the boys, not looking to take something new
home—only yourself, & perhaps a memory or two
for the week. After the club closed its doors & feet-
swelled-liquored-bodies poured hood-romance onto street,
you stumbled onto another parking lot where shadow-hued
earth music spewed out the trunks of cars loud enough to move
concrete & dim the moon's light between bass drops, between *boom*
boom boom & doom doom doom, Hennessey confidence, aromatic croons
of sweet, sweet Swisher Sweets:
 (   )
 (   )

SOME THINGS

You missed Nate-Relle's prison release party. He was doing well: a good job with good hours, a good woman who cooked regularly, he hooped regularly, spoke well of his baby's mom, maintained his prison physique.

You missed Kobe's retirement, much like MJ's, except The Lake Show tanked to get next year's ;pick. Kobe practically flamingoed himself through the league: wavin' goodbye at every stop, peacocked at standing ovations, injury-prone and cheer-struck. But a Mamba is a Mamba regardless, still dangerous and filled with venom. He dropped sixty before riding into the sunset: into Hollywood Boulevard: the pink of the city.

You missed Obama's visit. You missed Dino headlining worldwide news (of course, it's not what you'd expect). It wasn't to cover the ceasefire brokered by rival gang members or the governor un-naming us the cause of debt. It was an attack meant to terrorize our smog-thick city, a city that can't be terrorized by smog or death.

You missed Nate-Relle's return to prison. One of them *Boyz N The Hood* moments: Doughboy ridin' 'round the city inundated with street lights, lookin' for them fools who shot Ricky, and found them before flashing lights found him. I bet you can imagine Relle in the backseat ready to make a break, like *Damn! And I'm on parole. Ain't this a bitch!*

You missed Prince's departure, but not the newness in heaven, the now bell-sleeved cherubs strumming electric guitars.

You missed spring: NCAA madness culminating in an end, marigolds arrayed in full color like lovers rising from beds with something more to say.

You missed Luke's gray hair, your brother-less brother, his act of first kindling: silver to a lining in the cloud. A bold act of defiance, a root track to memory, a new birth.

The Necessity of Poetry

after Charles Simic

God made the mosquito so men would not be idle.
Cats are habitual like siestas in Spain.

I think more about people when they are gone.
I guess in some strange way that makes me a historian.

I'm told it takes a split second for butterflies to flap their wings.
Even less for a crocodile to bat its eyes, then it's over.

If a mosquito crosses the street, I will not ask his intentions.
For he knows in absolute he is as good as dead.

My wife's eyes are sometimes a hint of sunflower;
they lie still near the ocean without distinction.

In this I learn lives are coral-reefed in reason.
Sometimes they marble into dilated moons.

Sundays are repetitious like greetings in Arabic.
I will spare you any humor of *shokolatah* and *haleeb*.

Somewhere between the Atlantic and God-knows-where,
my black body metastasized into thick globs of goo.

I sprouted wings, shed my legs, my sickle cell anemia,
and became a mosquito presence in far-off lands.

Here, every man carries along sweat and racket.
He waves it, and every name becomes Aim and Fire.

The average honeybee beats its wings 270 times per second,
roughly six lightning bolts striking earth with their vein.

Six babies are born globally every 240 minutes.
A bullet travels 900 meters per second—aimed at you, times two—

Never once did I explain to the child why he's dying—
why his mosquito presence fell to earth like dry rain.

If Amichai were alive, he'd say,
I watched you grow into sunflower,

mature to age of bar mitzvah, develop in oblong
twitterpations—seal it with a kiss.

Then I'd see you in the street. Eyes like stop
signs, bleached red from war.

On His way to Jerusalem, Jesus, being hungry,
sees a tree without fruit—curses it.

In its unpreparedness,
it withers away.

Underneath the shade trees of Europe,
refugees wait for bread and country.

I join them trailside, sit up into the wee hours
of the night to recount old memories in the faces of card decks:

Oh yeah, now that Sandra—Sandra was a pure queen of hearts.
Tamir—Tamir was my ace. Big Mike—now that joker was cool as hell.

And as day breaks over our flightless bodies, we rise
like static from Van de Graaffs I touched as a child.

FLIGHT

\ 'flīt \ *from the Merriam-Webster Dictionary*

an act or instance of passing / [without] use of wings / a bee['s] ability / to fly / natural to birds / [short-lived] / through or through[out] space / earth / atmosphere / [by appointment with] an arrow / a rocket / the moon / the distance covered in such swift movement[s] / made by or in Transatlantic flight / an [un]scheduled trip at noon / that is making a trip [t]hey boarded a group of similar beings / or objects / flying through the air together / a continuous series of landing / or floor to another series resembling a flight / a unit of the US / [a]ir / [f]orce / squadron / a balloon / [a] shuttle / a Chicago / [a Cleveland / a St. Louis / a Baltimore] / flight to Mars / a group of similar things flying through the air together / an extraordinary display / to rise / settle / or flock / an act or instance of running / away

How I Survived

I stayed in late nights.
I shot late-night hoops.
I perfected windmills
and tomahawks.
I let my knees burn holes
in her mother's carpet.
I mixed Top Ramen
with blood sausage, Jesus
with mint juice.
I developed foresight
and bad omens, packed
Juicy Fruit, a sixth sense.
I avoided gaggles of geese,
murders of crows,
and uttered no language.
I left when it was time
to leave. I arrived too late.
I prayed before I walked.
I prayed before I prayed.
I focused my gaze
upon the ground.
I never gazed too long.
I honored my father and mother.
I had a father and mother.
I ran errands. I ran home.
I completed chores.
I didn't shoot. I shot

the breeze. I learned to clown
and mean mug. I listened
for rain. I listened for gun shots.
I hoped to God they didn't
figure me out. I didn't hang up
the phone. I hung up the phone.
She had a nice figure,
so I figured her yours.
I locked the storm door
when there were no storms,
and if someone knocked,
I wasn't quick to answer.
I moved away. I moved back.
I moved away again.
I remembered what to forget.
I wrote this poem.

PANTOUM

Let us believe for a moment that
in this poem there is no suffering,
and the white sheet is still freshly folded,
tucked away inside a dimly lit ambulance because

in this poem there is no suffering,
and the boy wearing his hood is enjoying his Skittles,
tucked away inside a dimly lit ambulance, because
he is receiving a generous ride home.

And the boy wearing his hood is enjoying his Skittles
next to the young man from St. Louis.
He is receiving a generous ride home
as well. Paramedics are joking with the boy wearing his hood

next to the young man from St. Louis.
One says, *What do you call a freshly folded white sheet?*
Paramedics are joking with the boy wearing his hood
as another man enters the ambulance. He overhears as

one says, *What do you call a freshly folded white sheet?*
The joke is interrupted
as another man enters the ambulance. He overhears as
the paramedic repeats the question.

The joke is interrupted.

A young lady enters, says she wouldn't be caught dead for failing to signal.

The paramedic repeats the question.

A twelve-year-old boy asks for a ride. He sits down next to

the young lady who said she wouldn't be caught dead for failing to signal.

She whispers the answer to

the twelve-year-old boy who asked for a ride.

He says, *I know the answer,*

whispers the answer, too.

Let us believe, for a moment, that.

NOTES

"Golden Shovel"
This form was invented by Terrance Hayes, who wrote a poem (titled "The Golden Shovel") using Gwendolyn Brooks's "We Real Cool" as direct inspiration. Hayes embedded the lines of Brooks's poem in his own, drawing the last word of his lines from hers, so that the source poem can be read vertically.

"Using the Laws of Motion to Explain Ferguson"
A found poem from the *Columbia Electronic Encyclopedia.*

"Unfinished Sonnet"
This poem's structure was influenced by William Shakespeare's Sonnet 126 (of the Fair Youth sequence), in which the final couplet is not included.

"The Necessity of Poetry"
Shokolatah and *haleeb* are English transliterations for the Arabic words meaning "chocolate" and "milk," which is how my wife and I (as an interracial couple) have often been referred to during our years in Middle Eastern countries.

"Flight"
A found poem from the *Merriam-Webster Dictionary.*

Other references and influences are cited in the epigraphs of individual poems.

ACKNOWLEDGMENTS

Sincere thanks to the editors and staff of the following publications in which the poems below previously appeared, sometimes as earlier drafts or under different titles:

Anomaly: "How to Make the World Beautiful" and "How We Are Made to Feel Small"

Chiron Review: "Pantoum on the Presidential Election"

Columbia Poetry Review: "Dear Basketball: A Posthumous Letter from St. Louis"

Frontier Poetry: "Unfinished Sonnet"

Ghost Town: "(More) Alternate Names for Black Boys"

HEArt Online: "Twelve Ways of Looking at Darkness"

International Poetry Review: "The Necessity of Poetry"

Pittsburgh Poetry Review: "Ghazal," "Pantoum," and "Using the Laws of Motion to Explain Ferguson"

Puerto del Sol: "A Love Poem"

Rattle: "How I Survived"

The Tishman Review: "Golden Shovel" and "Midway"

Third Wednesday: "We Sing"

"My Being-Black Dilemma" was the "What Rough Beast" poem for May 14, 2017, hosted by Indolent Books (www.indolentbooks.com).

"Twelve Ways of Looking at Darkness" was included in *Best "New" African Poets: 2016 Anthology* (African Books Collective, 2016), edited by Tendai Rinos Mwanaka and Daniel da Purificação.

"The Necessity of Poetry," "Pantoum," and "Pantoum on the Presidential Election" appeared in the anthology *Misrepresented People: Poetic Responses to Trump's America* (NYQ Books, 2018), edited by María Isabel Alvarez & Dante Di Stefano.

To Major Jackson, for seeing. Thank you for choosing *Flight* as the winner of the 2018 Sunken Garden Poetry Prize.

Thank you, Jeffrey Levine, Kristina Marie Darling, Marie Gauthier, and the team at Tupelo for your vision and acceptance. Thank you, Ann Aspell, for your perspective. Thank you, fellow poet and incredible editor, Jim Schley, for your patience, candor, and illumination.

Gratitude goes to the University of Alaska–Anchorage's MFA Program, for giving me a chance and for believing. To my fellow MFAers, for their voices and for making me feel at home. To the wonderful poetry and prose professors who brought life to every class, workshop, and nightly reading. To Dr. David Stevenson, Jenny Murray, and Kathleen Witkowska Tarr for their careful preparation every residency. To my mentors: Anne Caston, Linda McCarriston, Zack Rogow, the late Eva Saulitis, and the late Derick Burleson for their wisdom and their poetry. Thanks to Elizabeth Bradfield for her thorough teaching and dedication, her patience and thoughtfulness, and for challenging me throughout.

To Seri Luangphinith, for introducing me to form.

To *Pittsburgh Poetry Review* for nominating "Using the Laws of Motion to Explain Ferguson" for a 2017 Pushcart Prize.

To judge Phillip Sterling and *Third Wednesday* for choosing "We Sing" as a winner in the publication's annual poetry contest.

Thanks goes to the poetry group to which my wife and I belong—for seeing these drafts long before they were polished. To our group's fearless leader, Alice Jennings, for taking us through writing prompt after writing prompt.

To my family, through blood and marriage, for their unconditional support, and for feeding us and housing us every summer and during my time in the MFA Program.

To my parents, for never abandoning their posts, for their sacrifice and love. Thank you, Mom, for sharing the Word which guides my soul. Thank you, Dad, for telling me to go back to school.

To my coach, mentor, and friend Michael O'Connor: thank you for your constant encouragement, your vision, and for believing enough for the both of us.

To San Bernardino and St. Louis, for raising me in your streets and providing me with an education outside of the institution.

To my wife—my best friend and teacher—my constant encouragement and inspiration: the morning that brings me joy each day.

Thank You, God, for giving me the opportunity to write these poems.

Jeremiah 29:11.

Other Books from Tupelo Press

Silver Road: Essays, Maps & Calligraphies (memoir), Kazim Ali

A Certain Roughness in Their Syntax (poems), Jorge Aulicino, translated by Judith Filc

Another English: Anglophone Poems from Around the World (anthology), edited by Catherine Barnett and Tiphanie Yanique

Personal Science (poems), Lillian-Yvonne Bertram

Everything Broken Up Dances (poems), James Byrne

One Hundred Hungers (poems), Lauren Camp

Almost Human (poems), Thomas Centolella

Land of Fire (poems), Mario Chard

New Cathay: Contemporary Chinese Poetry (anthology), edited by Ming Di

Calazaza's Delicious Dereliction (poems), Suzanne Dracius, translated by Nancy Naomi Carlson

Gossip and Metaphysics: Russian Modernist Poetry and Prose (anthology), edited by Katie Farris, Ilya Kaminsky, and Valzhyna Mort

Poverty Creek Journal (memoir), Thomas Gardner

Leprosarium (poems), Lise Goett

My Immaculate Assassin (novel), David Huddle

Darktown Follies (poems), Amaud Jamaul Johnson

Dancing in Odessa (poems), Ilya Kaminsky

A God in the House: Poets Talk About Faith (interviews), edited by Ilya Kaminsky and Katherine Towler

Third Voice (poems), Ruth Ellen Kocher

The Cowherd's Son (poems), Rajiv Mohabir

Marvels of the Invisible (poems), Jenny Molberg

Canto General (poems), Pablo Neruda, translated by Mariela Griffor and Jeffrey Levine

The Ladder (poems), Alan Michael Parker

Ex-Voto (poems), Adélia Prado, translated by Ellen Doré Watson

The Life Beside This One (poems), Lawrence Raab

Intimate: An American Family Photo Album (hybrid memoir), Paisley Rekdal

The Voice of That Singing (poems), Juliet Rodeman

Dirt Eaters (poems), Eliza Rotterman

Good Bones (poems), Maggie Smith

Swallowing the Sea (essays), Lee Upton

feast gently (poems), G.C. Waldrep

Legends of the Slow Explosion: Eleven Modern Lives (essays), Baron Wormser

See our complete list at www.tupelopress.org